La\\

Transform You~ ~~~~ ~~~ ~~~~~~~~ ~~~~~~~~ - The Basics for Beginners

By Ris Jackson

If you like my book, please leave a positive review on Amazon. I would appreciate it a lot. Thanks! This is the link:

Leave your review here. Thank you!

Contents

Introduction

On the off chance that you've never utilized the Law of Attraction (LoA) before, you may ponder what it is, the reason such huge numbers of individuals trust it is valid, and how you can use it to your advantage. Luckily for you, this book is intended to answer these kinds of questions; and to provide you with an abundance of practical examples and uses that you can use straight away.

Be that as it may, before we go any further, we should try to answer these questions in the least difficult way that is possible:

What is the Law of Attraction (LoA)?

The LoA was formalized by the School of New Thought; despite that, there is some evidence that it has been around for a long time before that. To sum things up, the LoA states that things that are similar will attract one to the other. That is, whether I think emphatically, and I focus on positive results, at that point my considerations will really pull in those positive results into my life.

Now, to start with, you may think this sounds like magic. You may laugh at attracting ideas into your life through positive musings alone. Although, in truth, this has an exceptionally useful significance. What's more, truth be told, the LoA prescribes particular manners by which you can change your life through activities, instead of just considerations.

But how so, you may be asking? It's basic. By changing your attitude to concentrate on what you need, as opposed to what you don't have, you will come to see the world in an unexpected way. Each idea you have will bring you nearer to your objective, instead of cutting you down and focusing you on what you may never have.

So, by using the LoA it keeps you concentrated on approaches to enhance your life, as opposed to detours that you may just perceive instead of actually being genuine. And with that, brings us to the next question.

Why do a lot of people believe it is true?

As I stated, the LoA has numerous down to earth suggestions for your life. It guides you to do particular things that if you want, can really help to change the course of your life. What's more, this is the reason why many individuals believe it to be true: Not just does it confirm what they have consistently accepted to be true, however after they set it in motion, they see the positive outcomes that it has; and these outcomes change their lives.

Undoubtedly, it is the unmistakable, tangible progress that individuals encounter once they have embraced the LoA that makes them solid supporters; and that urges them to get the message out to others.

How Might You Use the LoA to Your Benefit?

The Law of Attraction has a lot of uses. It can be used to accomplish objectives. It can be used to enhance your financial circumstances. It can be used to get an advancement at work. Also, it can be used to enhance your relationships and connections with people.

The LoA is intense and valuable. It can change a man who is battling with his vocation and who feels as though he can never encounter accomplishment into a self-assured person who is prepared to finish his objectives; and won't let anything venture in his direction.

Chapter 1: Law of Attraction – An Overview

In what manner Should You Use It?

You now have some sort of idea of what the LoA is and why many individuals have embraced it. In any case, before we advance into the book, it's a good idea to give a stronger insight behind the LoA.

The LoA isn't just an announcement about fascination, however it is likewise a recommendation for how we should consider circumstances in our lives. Specifically, it urges us to consider abundance rather than scarceness. For example, think about the accompanying four circumstances. Choose whether you have an abundance or scarce mentality.

1. You're choosing whether to assist a business colleague with a project that he may be thinking of undertaking. You realize that it can possibly be fruitful; and you realize that you can help him to implement it. Be that as it may, you choose not to do

it. You choose that a little piece of your client base covers with his—and you would prefer not to lose even a solitary client to him.

2. You're choosing whether to begin an affiliate program to promote your new item, yet you're demoralized by the way that you have never done this. Rather than seeking out help from those who could help you, you conclude that it likely won't work out, so you don't do it.

3. You just began another business. You need to lease an office, with the goal that you have a place to send your workers. You realize this is a major risk, but instead of letting this get you down, you refuse to see it as a problem and rather push forward, resolved to influence it to work regardless of how hard it might appear to be at first.

4. You're choosing whether to do something nice for your significant other (spouse). You realize that you could make her/his life less demanding by helping out for her/him, however you at last choose not to.

Rather, you choose to hold the offer, with the goal that you can offer to do it as a negotiating tool for something in return.

After reading these cases, would you be able to see the distinction between a "abundance" outlook and "scarcity" attitude? Would you be able to perceive how the LoA guides you to think and carry on in a way that will produce mutuality and graciousness from others?

What's more, can you now see how following the LoA guides you not to stress constantly over being exploited; and not to carry on with your existence with the objective of extracting each and every penny and support from every other person, while doing nothing for them in return?

These are imperative things to see and to comprehend about the LoA in the event that you ever want to practice it effectively; and receive the benefits that it offers.

How Do You Know It Works?

Many individuals propose that you shouldn't stress over whether the LoA is working. You shouldn't stress whether or not thinking with a positive mind and keeping up a wealthy outlook creates better outcomes for you.

However, I disagree with this idea. Likewise, with everything you do throughout everyday life, business, and individual connections, it's vital to assess, regardless of what you are doing, what it actually has. It's not just importnat to do this, so you can refine your approach, yet in addition so you can choose whether or not what you're doing is extremely working by any means.

This is additionally valid with the LoA, regardless of what individuals may tell you.

Now, to start with, you may consider this to be kind of a contradiction. You may think about how you can at the same time be certain and accepting while likewise keeping up a level of doubt. But it really is completely possible.

How might you do this? Begin by setting a time for testing. Give yourself, say, 3 months. In this timeframe, submit yourself to following the Law of Attraction.

Amid this trial period, don't let anything stand amongst you and your objectives. Think decidedly and concentrate on accomplishing those objectives, as opposed to concentrating on the things that can keep you from accomplishing them.

Additionally, during that trial period, embrace the "abundance" attitude. Try not to stress over "winning" each social collaboration; and don't concentrate on extracting every single dollar from your clients, your business accomplices, and your companions.

To put it plainly, carry on as you would on the off chance that you had just accomplished your objectives. On the off chance that you were as rich, appealing, amiable, refined and astute as you wished to be, would you rub for each and every dollar? Obviously, you wouldn't. What's more, in the event that you ever need to arrive, you shouldn't act along these lines, either.

In this way, give yourself a trial period of around 3 months, put your everything into it, and see what happens. I ensure that living richly, thinking decidedly and helpfully, and providing for others without expecting something consequently will change your life, your business, and your connections emphatically.

Why Cynicism is Bad

With regards to the LoA, many individuals wrongly believe that suspicion is awful. However, in truth, there's nothing amiss with wariness. There's nothing amiss with thoroughly considering an arrangement before we make it. Furthermore, there's nothing amiss with pondering whether berries we picked in the timberland are eatable or noxious. Wariness is essential and can keep us alive and enhance how our organizations work.

Then again, criticism is a totally unique creature. When we persuade ourselves that nothing can be great, that nothing can work out well, and that everything in our lives is fixed against us, we buckle under something that is exceptionally in opposition to the LoA. In particular, we overlook attempting to draw in positive things into our lives through representation and activity; and we rather pester the things that have turned out badly.

On the off chance that you are not kidding about rehearsing the LoA to accomplish your objectives, to repair and reinforce your connections, and to end up noticeably fruitful in business or at work, at that point skepticism is the principal thing that must go. Furthermore, you should supplant it with a perpetual and determined readiness to conquer challenges.

Why Focus and Visualization is Important

The Law of Attraction recommends that in the event that we concentrate on positive things, at that point positive things will be pulled in into our lives. This is the reason adherents of LoA push that we put aside time amid the day to concentrate on the things that we need and envision them coming into our lives.

As another expert of the LoA, you should start putting aside time amid the day. You should begin by spending a few hours to plainly characterize your objectives. What's more, when you do this, don't just think about getting a specific measure of cash, yet figure principally about how you will utilize it (i.e. to improve your family's life, to get that house you generally needed, and so forth.).

After you have characterized your objectives, you ought to spend no less than a half hour every day doing nothing other than concentrating on them and imagining them happening. It might appear to be over the top at to begin with, yet actually, it is a technique that numerous expert competitors and fruitful businesspersons do all the time.

When you have done this a couple of times, you will comprehend why it bodes well. It encourages you to concentrate where it ought to be: to be specific, on accomplishing your objectives. It likewise causes you to stroll through your objectives deliberately, well ordered through representation. This is vital, as it will enable you to shape a particular arrangement about how you to can beat issues and accomplish objectives, regardless of how troublesome they may appear.

The most effective method to Create an Environment for Focus and Visualization

We've now settled that concentration and representation is an essential piece of applying the LoA. In the event that you can concentrate on your objectives, on the off chance that you can envision them happening, and you can acknowledge their occurrence, at that point you can apply the LoA effectively and receive the individual and material rewards that take after.

With this stated, it is vital to consider how you can enhance your concentration and reinforce your representation methods. You can begin by utilizing the accompanying procedures, which are known to enhance attitude, quiet nerves, and enable you to think:

1. Consume incense or light a fragrance based treatment flame. Pick an aroma that will stimulate you and center you, as opposed to dulling your faculties or putting you to rest. Aromas, for example, peppermint, grapefruit, or vanilla will finish this objective. Once the fragrance has filled the room, close your eyes and concentrate on your objectives. Endeavor to envision how they will happen; and feel open and tolerating as they do.

2. Get a back rub. A back rub can extricate up your muscles and influence you to feel casual and quiet. This will make it simple for you to concentrate your brain on just a single thing—to be specific, the procedure by which you will accomplish your objective.

3. Scrub down with diminish lighting. This will place you in a tranquil situation far from other individuals, where you can unwind and center. Focus your brain on just a single objective and how you will accomplish it.

4. Practice contemplation. A standout amongst other known strategies for concentrating on one idea just is contemplation. Figuring out how to ruminate better will convert into better utilization of the LoA. So, center and representation are essential parts of honing the LoA. Thus, in the event that you need to rehearse LoA accurately, at that point you have to discover approaches to center and envision better.

Step by step instructions to Avoid Bad Thoughts

As I said before, negativity can be dangerous to our utilization of the LoA. It can keep us from investing more energy by persuading us that things are impractical. Furthermore, it can keep us from concentrating on a thought and completing.

Hence, it is critical for us to keep terrible, pessimistic musings away when we are genuinely endeavoring to hone the Law of Attraction. Rather, we should concentrate on thoughts that are sure and that fortify our vision without bounds.

How might we do this? There are various diverse ways. I recommend only a couple beneath:

1.   Find Ways to Snap Out of Bad Thoughts

On the off chance that you end up strengthening terrible musings with all the more awful considerations, you need to discover some approach to break free from the cycle. Clinicians frequently recommend utilizing Cognitive Behavioral Therapy (CBT) systems in circumstances like this.

One regularly recommended CBT system includes wearing a versatile band around your wrist. When you begin to experience negative contemplations, snap that versatile band. That quick, physical input can help you to shock out of a cycle of negative considerations; and afterward start to settle your consideration on something unique.

Different strategies include suspending what you are doing at the time and accomplishing something unique. For example, on the off chance that you are in your desk area at work and you are taking a gander at an enormous pile of papers, you may start to feel discouraged and overpowered. Rather than staying there and gazing at the papers, get up and enjoy a speedy reprieve. Snatch an espresso or converse with somebody in an adjacent work area. This can break the cycle of cynicism before it starts.

2.   Avoid Places that Generate Bad Thoughts

In your everyday encounters, you have most likely perceived that specific spots cause awful contemplations. Maybe there was an occasion in the past where you fizzled at something startlingly. Or on the other hand maybe something terrible happened to you and your family; and at whatever point you go by a specific place, you think about that awful idea.

From here on out, it's a great opportunity to begin driving those spots out of your life. In the event that a place makes you miserable and there is almost no you can do to defeat that distress, at that point don't visit it any longer. Take an alternate course to work. To put it plainly, maintain a strategic distance from wherever that can put you on the way to ending up progressively negative.

3.   Carefully Choose and Maintain Relationships

On the off chance that you have companions who always debase you, question your capacities, or affront your thoughts, it's a great opportunity to make new companions. While it's a decent to have a cynic in the group to bob thoughts off of, it is once in a while help to have a critic around who can do nothing other than discover many (doubtful) manners by which your thoughts may come up short.

It finishes nothing; and it keeps you from keeping up your positive musings. In this way, every once in a while, assess your connections. Choose whether the companions you have related yourself with are enhancing your life and fortifying your prosperity; or whether they are basically dragging you down.

In short, the LoA can be outlined in three stages: to start with, ponder what it is that you really need most. Second, concentrate just on that thing and picture how you will draw in it into your life. What's more, third, be open and tolerating of that thing that you need most, regardless of whether you at first intuitively fear finishing it.

Past that, rehearsing the LoA adds up to practicing center and perception. It additionally expects you to think as far as plenitude, instead of shortage. In the accompanying parts, I will talk about particular manners by which you can apply the LoA to enhance your life.

Chapter 2: LoA and Relationships

LoA and Love

When you first observe the Law of Attraction, you likely did not quickly acknowledge how it connected to love and connections. Rather, you may consider it to be a device, which you can use to remove material riches from the world.

Truth be told, the LoA has a considerable measure to say in regards to connections. It not just proposes how you should approach potential accomplices outside of connections, yet it likewise recommends how you ought to cooperate with them inside connections. In the accompanying areas, we will consider the manners by which you can apply the LoA to sentimental connections.

Step by step instructions to Find the Right Person

On the off chance that you consider the LoA for more than a couple of minutes, it'll turn out to be clear precisely how it recommends that you locate the "right" individual for you. Rather than fixating on somebody you definitely know, yet who does not enjoy you—or hopping into an association with the most readily accessible individual, what you ought to do is picture it's identity that you wish to be with.

Consider this long and hard. Picture this individual. Should this individual have fundamentally the same as interests to your own? Or on the other hand should this individual have altogether different interests, so you can impart your own particular altogether different interests to each other?

Answer these questions and consolidate them into your representation. Also, once you do that, start to consider how you will meet this individual. Will you meet at work? Will you meet at a religious occasion? While you meet at gathering that is identified with your enthusiasm? Start to settle these thoughts; and afterward concentrate on your arrangement precisely.

You won't not feel it instantly, but rather something interesting will begin to happen. As you meet potential accomplices, you'll invest less energy concentrating on appearance and additional time concentrating on your vision. You will review what it is that you needed most; and rapidly decide if a potential individual would be a decent match for you.

Besides, once you do find that individual who fulfills your vision, you will realize that it is genuinely who you need to be with. What's more, rather than trembling at the possibility of asking him or her out on the town, you will feel sure that you have settled on the correct choice; and you will experience no difficulty doing it.

Step by step instructions to Improve Romantic Relationships

The LoA makes particular proposals about sentimental connections, as well. Typically, we disclose to ourselves that haggling is an imperative piece of connections. We expect that on the off chance that we don't discover approaches to make our accomplice obligated to us, they will never energetically get things done for us.

Lamentably, this can prompt extremely troubled connections over the long haul. Today, we may accomplish something that puts us at favorable position in respect to our accomplice, however tomorrow, they may trap us into accomplishing something that we would prefer not to do.

Rather, take after the exhortation of the LoA and break free from this cycle. Make it a point to dependably do kind things for your accomplice without asking or expecting any response at all.

At first, you may think that its tacky to do these exercises. For example, you may wind up clearing the house and washing the dishes more than you may incline toward at first. Be that as it may, after some time, as you perceive how your accomplice reacts to your magnanimous deed, you will like it and need to do it intentionally.

Significantly, as your accomplice watches this, he or she will need to react and accomplish something proportional for you. This positive cycle can possibly altogether enhance the nature of your relationship; and, specifically, to enable you to break free from the blow for blow cycles that frequently create out of generally great connections.

Step by step instructions to Deal with Relationships that Don't Work

At a few focuses in our lives, we wind up seeing someone that just aren't intended to be. The planned life partner may have uncontrollably unique center convictions. Or on the other hand might need to accomplish genuinely inconsistent objectives.

After some time, the relationship may decline. We may wind up battling with somebody who once appeared like an imminent accomplice over genuinely trifling things. Rather than going separate ways and proceeding onward with our particular lives, rather we battle severely and end the relationship on exceptionally poor terms.

Applying the LoA, we can see that there are great other options to an intense separation, as well. For example, rather than spending every day fortifying it is inescapable that things will deteriorate; and that it is unavoidable that the separate will at last occur after a major battle, we can concentrate rather on something different.

We can concentrate on the relationship slowing down. We can picture how we will part from the relationship without things getting intense and without offending of the other individual.

It may sound extraordinary and surprising, however there are approaches to end connections genially and without hard emotions; and utilizing the LoA can be one of those ways.

The Most Effective Method to Move on After a Failed Relationship

Not just have we as a whole encountered a relationship that commonly did not work, but rather we have all accomplished misfortune at some point. We're really infatuated with the other individual, yet the other individual essentially needs no part in our life.

This can be exceptionally wrecking; and a few people who encounter it don't completely recoup from the separation for quite a long time to come. On the off chance that you wind up in this circumstance, it is essential to infer what the LoA would propose: positive musings pull in positive results; and negative contemplations draw in negative results.

On the off chance that you concentrate just on the absence of the individual you once adored beyond a reasonable doubt, these contemplations will just strengthen themselves. You will turn out to be progressively adverse; and progressively centered around this individual who is not any more a piece of your life.

Rather, what you ought to do is concentrate on recouping, balancing out, and discovering approaches to fill the void in your life that that individual left. You may do this by taking a break from dating and defining business related objectives. Or then again you may concentrate on finding another planned accomplice to replace the other.

Whatever you do, it is insightful to review the lessons of the LoA as you do it. Remember positive contemplations; and concentrate on finding another, reasonable accomplice, as opposed to lamenting unendingly with the prospect that you will never recoup what is pitifully lost.

Companionship

With regards to connections, the LoA has more to state. It not just trains you on the best way to act inside sentimental connections, yet in addition recommends what you may foul up in fellowships.

At to start with, your intuitive answer may be that you're doing nothing amiss with fellowships, yet when you consider this more extended, you may reach an alternate conclusion. Simply think about the greater part of the companions you have lost in the past who were steady, kind, and adoring. For what reason did you lose those companions? What's more, wouldn't your life be better on the off chance that they had never vanished in the first place? In the areas underneath, we will consider how the LoA recommends that you make and look after fellowships.

a.   How to Make Friends

As anyone might expect, the LoA is certain as far as how it recommends that you make companions. As opposed to proposing that you ought to randomly fall into fellowships and afterward keep up them once started, it recommends that concentration, perception, and objective setting are vital.

That is, as opposed to just enabling companions to become alright in your life, you should begin by defining objectives. You ought to conclude that you need to make companions; and you should consider who they will be. Will they have comparative occupations? Will they have a similar instruction or preparing? Will they have the capacity to help you positively? Will you have the capacity to respond?

When you answer these questions and fix yourself on an objective, the time has come to center and envision. Envision these companions; and picture them coming into your life, as you meet them and cooperate with them in your day by day life.

Besides, as you meet new individuals, fuse them into your perceptions. Perceive how you envision them to assume a part in your life. Do they enhance it? Do they improve you a man? Do they empower you to do things that you generally proved unable?

Obviously, you can't know the greater part of this data ahead of time. As you take in more about a man, you additionally take in more about the part that individual may play in your life. Thus, you should re-imagine and settle on these choices as you go.

Keep in mind that the LoA would recommend that you experience a similar procedure for existing companions. Basically on the grounds that you have known a man for quite a while doesn't really mean they are a positive effect on your life.

In the event that you can imagine your life enhancing with the steady antagonism of a specific companion, you may need to either urge that companion to wind up noticeably more positive; or discover approaches to remove yourself from the companion, so you don't end up ending up progressively critical and negative yourself.

b.   How to Become Closer with Friends

Notwithstanding discovering companions, you will likewise need to utilize the LoA to assess and fortify existing connections. As you probably are aware well, on the off chance that you don't put enough exertion into a fellowship, you will float separated from the other individual; and may inevitably go your own specific manner, never to return.

Consequently, you will need to utilize the LoA to envision the results of your kinships. Concentrate on which companions are important and could sensibly be great, long haul companions. What's more, consider additionally who does not assume a critical part in your life; or who as a rule assumes a mind-boggling negative part.

So, choose its identity you need to get nearer to; it's identity you are unverifiable about; and its identity you might want to remove yourself from. From that point, utilize the energy of perception to decide how your connections will change.

Envision yourself reaching your negative companions less much of the time. Or on the other hand envision how you can communicate with them in ways so they assume an entirely positive part in your life. In any case, whatever you do, don't imagine yourself in the position you are in now where a tirelessly negative companion cuts you down and disheartens you, and you don't make a move.

For those companions you wish to get nearer to, concentrate on manners by which you can move them nearer. Rather than enigmatically perceiving how they assume a part in your life, envision how you may control the part that they play in your life, with the goal that both you are in an ideal situation for it.

c.   How to Mend Broken Relationships

At long last, the LoA has a great deal to state with regards to broken connections. For example, on the off chance that you have had a dropping out with a dear companion, however need to retouch the circumstance, the LoA might be the correct apparatus for the activity.

As usual, begin by settling the objective: to retouch your broken relationship. Next, envision how you will do it. Will you contact the companion and apologize for something you have done? Or on the other hand will you just be tolerating of something they did before, despite the fact that it hurt you profoundly at the time?

Stroll through this procedure in your psyche. Envision how it will happen, how the other individual may react, and how you will stay with things until the point that everything is worked out.

Furthermore, convey your plenitude outlook to the table when you contact your old companion. Try not to plan to win a clash of words. What's more, don't get ready to be vindicated in your earlier position or in your convictions.

Rather, recollect your objective: to recover your companion. And after that achieve it through perception, center, and finish.

At last, recollect the last advance of the LoA: you should be open and tolerating of the outcomes. In the event that you even somewhat start to question whether you genuinely need your old companion back, at that point you may disrupt the objective before you ever find the opportunity to acknowledge it.

Section Summary

In this section, we've given an extensive diagram of how to apply the Law of Attraction to connections. Regardless of whether it's a sentimental relationship gone amiss or a companionship that should be finished gently, the LoA has certain directions about what you ought to do.

As I've said a few times all through the section, there are two essential things to consider while applying the

LoA. The first is the three stage process, which is regular to all LoA applications:

Step #1: Think about what you genuinely want. And afterward submit yourself to accepting that thing that you need most. For this situation, it may patch a broken companionship, finishing a relationship, or finding your life partner.

Step #2: Visualize how you will get that result once a day. Here, this may mean envisioning your life partner, who he or she will be, the place he or she will work, and what kind of foundation that individual will have.

Step #3: Open yourself to accepting the result, to finding that mate, to making another companion, or to retouching a broken kinship. As unusual as it might appear, we are frequently our greatest foe with regards to accepting the things we trust we need most. When they are at long last in achieve, we expect that we may not genuinely need them, so we subliminally push them away. The LoA recommends that you completely should not do this in the event that you need to see those outcomes.

Notwithstanding the three-advance process, it is indispensable that you carry an attitude of wealth with you wherever you rehearse the LoA. That is, rather than concentrating on the dread that you may "lose" something in a companionship or sentimental relationship, concentrate on what you can pick up by going into an all the more commonly valuable condition of the relationship.

Chapter 3: LoA and Money

Step by step instructions to Start a Business

With regards to business, you may be reluctant to apply the LoA. You may ask whether it may be more reasonable to leave the LoA in your own life; and concentrate on separating benefits in your business life.

Actually, however, the LoA doesn't quit working essentially on the grounds that you concluded that you're finished with it. It's an all inclusive rule that applies not exclusively to your own life and to your objective setting, however to your business and work life. Furthermore, in case you're willing to utilize it to make a business, you may simply be shocked at how great your outcomes end up being.

All in all, with regards to beginning a business, what can the LoA say? Above all else, it urges you to hone center, perception, and wealth. How about we perceive how you can do each of these.

1. Focus

With regards to beginning a business, center is basic. Without center, you will get yourself lost in the clamor of business while critical signs disregard your head. That is, you will invest energy pursuing around deadlock thoughts; you will dump cash into ventures and afterward immediately abandon them; and you will enable accomplishment to evade you at all conceivable open doors.

Hence, with regards to business, rehearse what the LoA recommends: set particular objectives and concentrate barely on them. Rather than investing no energy drafting the objectives and the greater part of your opportunity working towards badly characterized objectives, concentrate on the objectives; and once you set them, don't let anybody or anything move you far from them.

2. Visualization

The LoA makes another proposal about how you should begin a business. You ought to do it by envisioning what your business will be, the means by which it will run, and how everything will meet up.

The cerebrum has a mind blowing ability to reenact occasions. What's more, you should utilize it to imagine how your business will create, develop, and change into a lucrative open door for you.

3. Abundance

The plenitude attitude is additionally essential. Numerous new entrepreneurs fail in favor of being modest. They hold back on the sign for the business; they deal representative wages as low as they can go; and they buy low quality materials from providers.

Therefore, huge numbers of them at last come up short. What's more, numerous others for all time wind up as independent companies with no development potential. The niggardliness and state of mind that they pass on is at last what they pull in when they procure help and experience clients.

With this stated, contemplate what the LoA proposes when about your new business. While it is astute to be thrifty while making a business, it is vital not to take that thriftiness to an overabundance level. Rather, act with the expectation to make a high caliber, helpful item for your clients; and they will react to you in kind.

The most effective method to Grow a Business

Notwithstanding educating you on the most proficient method to begin a business, it is likewise conceivable to utilize the LoA while managing the extension of your business. Give me a chance to give you a few cases of how you may utilize the LoA in these circumstances:

Illustration #1: Hiring a Graphic Design Person

You will extend your Internet-based business by making another, however related website. What's more, you require a logo for that site. When it comes time to make the logo, you eventually choose to procure somebody for the activity. At to start with, you don't know the amount to pay them. However, inevitably, you choose to hold back. You reason that you don't have the $50 to pay for the logo, since you may never recoup the cash if the site does not succeed.

Subsequently, you buy a logo for $5; and, without a doubt, it's not a big deal. Tragically for you, this is precisely what guests additionally think when they see it. They consider you to be somebody who is so un-invested in her own particular business that she isn't willing to pay even $50 for a great logo. Subsequently, they ignore you for the opposition.

In the event that you had connected the LoA, your outcomes would have been significantly extraordinary. You would have understood that fascination is an imperative piece of PR. Your contemplations, activities, and the way you pass on your business to others shapes how they will react to it. What's more, therefore, you can begin off by "being shabby"; and afterward buy a superior plan of action once you've profited. You need to begin off by passing on wealth; and after that receive the benefits of fascination.

Illustration #2: Hiring an Affiliate Manager

Your business is right now at an intersection. It has extended the extent that the present plan of action will allow. Also, the essential imperative is your opportunity. Specifically, you find that it takes no less than 20 hours every week to deal with your members.

A companion of yours proposes that you enlist an associate director. For as meager as $10/hr, ($200/wk), you could discover by one means or another who will do these undertakings for you, liberating you up to only invest your energy growing your business.

On a fundamental level it sounds incredible, yet when you consider it more, it alarms you. The prospect of paying somebody a settled compensation every week appears to be alarming. Imagine a scenario where you don't profit to pay yourself in the wake of paying the associate supervisor. For sure in the event that you some way or another observe the best approach to be more proficient, so you can decrease the measure of time that you go through with partners; and rather center your vitality somewhere else.

At last, you choose not to contract a partner administrator. You choose that once your business winds up noticeably effective and you end up plainly rich, you can employ a subsidiary chief, with the goal that you don't need to spend your day doing such paltry errands.

Subsequently, your business never develops. The limitation on development has dependably been your opportunity; and with a lot of it bound up on offshoot administration errands, you have almost no time left finished to pull in new customers and grow new items.

Once more, this is a case of you not utilizing the LoA. Had you utilized the LoA, you would have understood that your shortage attitude was obstructing advance. That is—rather than employing the subsidiary director once you "got rich," you ought to have been procuring the associate chief to get rich.

Obviously, notwithstanding these illustrations, you can consider numerous more manners by which the LoA can manage your reasoning with regards to business development. Simply make sure to concentrate on wealth; and that is the thing that you will draw in into your business.

The most effective method to Create Business Partnerships

One thing that numerous new entrepreneurs disregard is the estimation of a decent business association. This is particularly valid for the individuals who don't comprehend and apply the LoA. In every association they have, their exclusive objective is to separate benefits and proceed onward before the other individual understands he's been cheated.

In actuality, on the off chance that you receive and take after the LoA in your business hones, at that point you ought to likewise take after its suggestions for business associations. That is, rather than regarding associations as an exercise in futility, understand that they contain the possibility to be substantially more than a one-time gig. What's more, understand that numerous organizations are made or lost construct just in light of associations with existing organizations.

Rather, concentrate painstakingly on each of your business associations. Picture how they will assume a part later on of your business. And afterward work with your business accomplices appropriately.

In the event that you imagine that a solid, long haul organization is conceivable, at that point cultivate a more grounded association with that accomplice.

Regard them as the plenitude outlook would recommend. That is, rather than straightforwardly passing on that you have no time for them or no enthusiasm for joining forces with them unless all advantages accumulate to you, rather regard them as though you have additional time; and as though you are available to ventures that may entirely profit them and not you.

Once more, recall that the embodiment of the LoA is concentrating on plenitude and energy. It comprises of imagining positive results precisely; and after that making an interpretation of those perceptions into solid activities.

This is the same here. In the event that you need to fashion associations, at that point you should first imagine them. Next, you should stay open to them and enthusiastically acknowledge them when they introduce themselves.

Also, all things considered, we will finish off this area on LoA and business. Keep in mind, the approach hasn't changed—just the topic has. In the event that you need to apply the LoA basically and accurately, you should simply set objectives, imagine them happening, and afterward acknowledge that those positive results when they happen.

LoA and the Workplace

For those of you who are not growing business people or prepared entrepreneurs, you may in any case find numerous utilizations of the LoA with regards to the working environment. Specifically, you can utilize the LoA to enhance your status inside your companion gathering, to get raises, to get advancements, and to catch openings that may somehow or another escape you. In this segment, we will think about each of these conceivable outcomes.

LoA and Getting a Promotion

Getting an advancement is precarious business. For the most part, it includes diligent work, bartering, and governmental issues. Luckily, you have an instrument that many don't have available to them: the Law of Attraction. Furthermore, you can apply it to guarantee that you get advanced. - 28 –

How is this? Underneath, we'll consider two diverse manners by which you can utilize the Law of Attraction to get an advancement:

Illustration #1: Using Focus and Visualization

Something that different the individuals who utilize the LoA from the individuals who don't is the capacity of LoA clients to remain concentrated on objectives. For the individuals who don't utilize it (and this may incorporate you as of recently), the association between their objectives and their activities isn't generally evident. Rather, they concentrate on one objective for a timeframe, battle to perceive how they can accomplish it, and after that move to the following.

Utilizing center and representation is a basic piece of guaranteeing that you accomplish your objective of getting advanced. Rather than abandoning yourself loose in an ocean of shifting desire and thoughts, you need to choose what it is that you need. That is section 1 of the LoA. What's more, you've officially chosen: you need an advancement.

Section 2 expects you to concentrate barely on that objective and imagine it happening. Could you? On the off chance that you can't, at that point you might need to reconsider whether you extremely needed the advancement in any case. On the off chance that you experience genuine protection, at that point you may need to really ask yourself whether the expansion in pay will be justified regardless of the expansion in obligations.

On the off chance that you can picture this procedure, at that point it is essential to do as such frequently. This will keep you concentrated on your objective; and it will help you to discover ways that you can pull in that advancement into your life.

One thing you will see as you go ahead and rehearse your representations is an increased feeling of familiarity with your objective. When you are grinding away, you will be profoundly aware of what you are doing; and you will consider how it influences your likelihood of getting an advancement.

At in the first place, this may appear like an awful thing, yet truth be told, it is a standout amongst other approaches to accomplish positive results. Rather than giving the world a chance to do however it sees fit you, you will assume responsibility and decide how the world will be formed by your vision.

Illustration #2: Persuading Co-Workers and Bosses

Notwithstanding utilizing the LoA to concentrate on and picture your advancement, you can likewise utilize the LoA in different approaches to induce colleagues and managers to battle for your advancement.

How might you do this? The short answer is that you can do as such by utilizing the energy of positive idea. The more extended answer is that honing the LoA in the work environment won't just make you a more successful laborer, however it will likewise urge others to crusade for your advancement.

The explanation behind this lies in the quintessence of the LoA approach: to concentrate only on the best way to defeat challenges, instead of on their reality itself. At to begin with, this may appear to be excessively idealistic to your colleagues, however as supervisors and associates alike observe you in real life, they will progressively come to value your approach.

Where others surrender and infer that a test is just unconquerable, you will keep wearing down the issue until the point that you at long last make an achievement. What's more, you will do this decisively on the grounds that you realize that the LoA works; and that, by utilizing it, you can't just make progress at last, yet use that accomplishment into an advancement.

With this stated, you now have two effective apparatuses available to you with regards to applying the LoA to get an advancement at work. We should now consider how you can utilize the LoA to enhance the state of your work environment.

Step by step instructions to Improve Your Relationship with Co-Workers

Another manner by which you can apply the LoA to your work environment is to enhance your association with your colleagues. At to begin with, you won't not think this is awfully critical, but rather indeed, it can have the effect between an extremely miserable, discouraging day at work and a pleasurable day at work.

Along these lines, rather than being ostensibly negative and criticizing towards your associates, discover approaches to enhance your associations with them. Be that as it may, before you do this, begin by persuading yourself that it is a beneficial objective, as the LoA educates. When you have persuaded yourself that it is advantageous to enhance your climate at work by creating more grounded associations with your colleagues, you would then be able to advance from that point.

The subsequent stage, obviously, is perception. You should envision how you will push ahead from your present position. You should draw an obvious conclusion in your brain by envisioning how you will turn out to be nearer with your collaborators; and how you will position yourself to be useful and inviting.

In short, rolling out these slight improvements can significantly affect your condition at work. Not exclusively will you anticipate seeing your colleagues, however you will likewise drop the attitude that you are altogether contending in zero-aggregate amusement. Also, you may think that its urging to go to work every day when you know you will be welcomed by companions who think about you, as opposed to individuals who are conspiring to grab that advancement in front of you.

The Most Effective Method to Enjoy Your Work Life More

In the case of nothing else, the LoA discloses to us that we have the ability to shape and reshape our lives. It trains us to concentrate on considerations and activities that are helpful for the certain objectives we set. What's more, to abstain from getting to be impeded in pessimism and speculative debacle situations.

Rather, what we ought to do is consider how we need to reshape our life, with the goal that it is better. We should consider how a test may be overcome, instead of fixating that the test exists in any case.

To put it plainly, we have to move far from negative musings. Also, we have to move towards positive, gainful, noteworthy contemplations. We require considerations that can advance us and give us heading, as opposed to ones that make us life in dread of disappointment.

Since the working environment is where we spend a lot of our waking hours (maybe 30 to 60 of them seven days), it's nothing unexpected that the way to enhancing our lives frequently lies in how cheerful we are with our function life.

Strikingly, however, the LoA doesn't really train us to "locate another activity" if the present one is giving finished fulfillment. Or maybe, it recommends that we should quit concentrating so barely on our disappointment. Rather, what we ought to do is concentrate on how that disappointment may be overwhelmed by our activities and state of mind.

Not exclusively does this approach help us to enhance our lives, yet it engages us to take control of things we typically let control us. For example, every day, we live in dread of numerous things that will occur at work; and, when they do, we will get ourselves chafed or exhausted.

Shockingly, the vast majority of us do little to endeavor to change these circumstances. Rather than concentrating on the issue and picturing a conceivable and positive arrangement, we basically offer in to its certainty, and invest the day fearing the energy when it will at long last appear.

In any case, in truth, we don't have. We can take control of our life. Also, we can do it utilizing the LoA. Starting now and into the foreseeable future, spend no less than 15 minutes every night imagining how you can enhance the accompanying workday. Concentrate on the things that you detest most; and utilize the capable test system that your cerebrum gives with a specific end goal to conquer those things.

Yet, furthermore, remember what the LoA claims: you will draw in that which you concentrate on. In this way, you may not just need to concentrate on drawing in these reasonable enhancements into your life, however you may likewise need to concentrate on pulling in the things that you do appreciate about your workday, as well. On the off chance that you can enhance these things, you will fear the coming workday less and less.

LoA and Personal Finance

With regards to the Law of Attraction, there are huge and vital things you can do with it. You can utilize it to make companions, to enhance sentimental relations, to get an advancement at work, or to begin another business. What you won't not understand is that it is likewise useful for little things, such as taking care of basic individual fund issues. In this area, we will consider how to utilize it accurately.

Instructions to Improve Your Finances with the LoA

At a certain point in the greater part of our individual lives, we've been in this circumstance: we're working constantly, however it just doesn't pay the bills. We're perseveringly behind on lease. We're experiencing difficulty making the auto installment. What's more, we're eating things we ordinarily wouldn't just in light of the fact that they were at a bargain at the market.

In those circumstances, we were most likely exceptionally aware of our neediness. We concentrated for the most part on what we needed; and it influenced us to feel frail and feeble. We felt as though even a modest change in our lives could influence the whole place of cards tumble to down.

Luckily, in case you're in this circumstance now, you now have the chance to utilize the LoA to receive yourself in return. Rather than concentrating on your neediness (which, as the LoA recommends, will just sire destitution), you can concentrate on something different.

Truth be told, you can overlook your destitution totally; and concentrate on what you can do. Furthermore, not surprisingly, it should all begin with an arrangement of objectives, which originate from watchful idea and core interest.

For example, what objectives would you be able to set that could lift you out of destitution and put you on track to ending up monetarily secure? Concentrate on this every day in a helpful and non-negative way. At long last, settle these objectives and stay with them.

When you have settled your objectives, begin to imagine how they will be figured it out. Envision that you are strolling through the procedure; and expect how you will react to challenges and succeed.

The majority of this is critical. It will set you up to act the majority of this out, all things considered, where difficulties will buffet you; and where you will be compelled to depend on possibility plants to explore through an entangled world.

At long last, as constantly open yourself to the acknowledgment of this objective. Find a sense of contentment with it; and don't self-undermine a decent result.

Step by Step Instructions to Apply the Principle of Abundance When You're Broke

It may sound conflicting, however the rule of plenitude doesn't quit applying just in light of the fact that you are poor. When you utilize the LoA to concentrate on circumstances where you confront plenitude, as opposed to shortage, that is exactly what you will pull in into your life after some time.

What's more, there require not be anything mysterious or unexplained about it. Or maybe, the fascination originates from your concentration, perception, and assurance. As opposed to concentrating on how poor you will be, you will concentrate on how you may push off your own destitution and end up plainly rich.

This redirection of thought can do ponders as far as keeping you concentrated on genuine, achievable objectives, as opposed to the dread of disappointment. So make sure to rehearse it, notwithstanding when the circumstances are hardest; and notwithstanding when the prospects are bleakest.

Section Summary

The Law of Attraction require not just assume a part in your social life. It can likewise be utilized to enhance your results in the working environment, with a business you claim, or in any individual or monetary wander you take. The way to getting everything to work is basically to take after the three-advance system I have rehashed all through this book: initially, settle an objective. Second, imagine yourself fulfilling that objective. What's more, third, open yourself to understanding that objective.

Chapter 4: LoA and Personal Growth

LoA and Goals

What's more, in case you're similar to the vast majority, you set objectives constantly, however you once in a while acknowledge them. Many individuals, for example, submit themselves to a specific New Year's determination, yet absolutely never complete. You might be liable of this, as well.

On the off chance that you have an enthusiasm for evolving this in figuring out how to guarantee that you finish your objectives—at that point the Law of Attraction can be an existence changer.

Why would that be? Since the LoA is about objectives and accomplishment. It contains an outstanding truth: that the distinction between the individuals who succeed and the individuals who fall flat is frequently an extremely thin edge. The ones who succeed were ready to remain with an objective for only somewhat more; and the ones who fizzled gave in.

With this stated, we should investigate two cases of how you can apply the LoA to objectives in your own life:

Case #1: Weight Loss

Maybe you've been endeavoring to lose 20 pounds for a considerable length of time, however have never succeeded. Previously, you've chosen to do it various circumstances, yet you essentially never finished. Utilizing the LoA, you would now be able to accomplish this objective with considerably less exertion, enduring, and inner battle.

You can begin by settling your emphasis on the objective: weight reduction. Conclude that it is something you have to do. Discover motivations to help this objective; and always help yourself to remember these reasons.

When you have really acknowledged that this objective is deserving of the battle it will bring, move into the perception stage. Envision how you will lose that weight. See yourself buckling down and the rec center; and settling on troublesome dietary decisions that require forfeit.

Besides, envision how rolling out these improvements will enhance your life. See yourself later on after you have thinned down. Do you feel more beneficial? Do you feel less unsure? Do you feel more appealing and fearless?

These are exceptionally vital things to see and to figure it out. What's more, there's no preferred method to do it over utilizing the LoA. Simply recollect: in the event that you need to draw in a slimmer adaptation of yourself into your life, at that point you should settle your psyche on that picture.

At last, open yourself to the acknowledgment of the objective. In those peculiar minutes where you all of a sudden uncertainty whether you truly need to be 20 pounds slimmer, push back and insist your unique objective. You have settled on the correct decision and you know it, so don't give clashing feels a chance to surprise your advance.

Case #2: Personal Growth

Every once in a while, we wind up noticeably exhausted with existing conditions and ponder what our lives may resemble on the off chance that we had invested the energy to build up an ability or take in a specialty. For example, you may consider how your life would be in the event that you had kept on playing the saxophone; or in the event that you had adapted more workmanship.

These are on the whole real longings; and every present us with a plausibility for self-awareness and more noteworthy life fulfillment. In any case, on the off chance that we ever need to encounter the joy of playing an instrument skillfully or honing another specialty expertly, at that point we should spend and push to enhance our abilities.

Luckily, the LoA clarifies unequivocally how we can do this. We can begin by genuinely choosing what we need to do it; and once we do that, we can settle it as our objective. For example, conclude that you need to play the saxophone.

Presently, if this not genuinely something you need to do, at that point don't make it an objective. Just make it an objective in the event that it is something you really need in your life; and on the off chance that it is genuinely something you accept will improve your life in unmistakable ways.

With your objective settled, imagine how you will achieve it. Will you hone three times each week? Will you rehearse early in the day or will you do it after work? Will you welcome your family to be a piece of it? Will you discover different performers and play your instrument with them?

At long last, open yourself to the acknowledgment of the objective. Envision that it is one year later on and you have turned into a refined sax player. What is your opinion about this vision? It is safe to say that you are uneasy with it? Do you unusually feel unsatisfied with it, as though you were genuinely inspired by the pursuit, not the acknowledgment?

All things considered, get over these sentiments of uneasiness. The last phase of the LoA includes getting to be plainly alright with the acknowledgment of your objectives. What's more, this is decisively what you need to do in the event that you wish to be effective.

LoA and Learning

One last subject we will consider is LoA and learning. This is essential since learning issues are frequently what keep individuals from being effective. Possibly they aren't willing to learn persistently and change as they learn; or they aren't willing to pick up something that will empower them to develop and settle on better choices.

With this stated, applying the LoA is an indistinguishable procedure from dependably. Begin by choosing what it is that you have to learn or how you have to change the procedure by which you learn (i.e. maybe you need to learn constantly, as opposed to discretely, as you do now).

When you have bound that objective, the procedure is the same than it was for any of the illustrations we have secured up to this point. Just picture the result; and after that open yourself to the acknowledgment of that learning and to the advantages it will bring.

Section Summary

In this concise section, we considered how the Law of Attraction can be connected to self-awareness. What's more, obviously, the appropriate response is the same as usual. Begin by binding the self-awareness objective. From that point, rehash the three-advance process until the point when you make progress.

Conclusion

All through this book, we have examined the Law of Attraction inside and out. You have seen the law itself, you took after its suggestions, and you have seen a wide exhibit of various illustrations that clarify correctly how you can apply it to your life.

You now realize that the Law of Attraction urges you to complete three things: 1) to set objectives; 2) to envision those objectives being completed; and 3) to acknowledge the realization of those objectives as it happens. It might appear to be weird or enchanted, yet rehashing this three-advance process is evidently effective; and carries with it the guarantee of a superior existence with more prominent material and individual achievement.

The other thing you've learned is the rule of plenitude, which manages how you should utilize the Law of Attraction. Regardless of whether it comes to business, your own life, or your objectives, you should concentrate on wealth, as opposed to shortage. Furthermore, the explanation behind doing as such is clear: you need to pull in wealth into your life, not shortage, so this is absolutely what you should settle your contemplations on.

Be that as it may, now that we've touched base now, whatever is left of the voyage is yours. It is dependent upon you to apply the LoA (or to not have any significant bearing it). It is dependent upon you to set objectives that you genuinely believe are deserving of your chance and exertion; and to complete these objectives utilizing representation and acknowledgment.

In the event that you can apply the LoA to your life effectively; and you can stay with it, you will locate the correct outcomes you looked for at first. Your life will enhance voluntarily; and your lacks and issues will gradually blur away from plain sight.

So begin today. Start your first objective setting session and choose what it is that you need to achieve most. When you are done with that, put some time aside today around evening time to concentrate on those objectives and picture how you will make them happen. At last, ensure you are genuinely open to the acknowledgment of your objectives, with the goal that you don't quietly disrupt them by undermining the objectives you have chosen.

Thanks again for buying my book. If you have a minute, please leave a positive review. You can leave your review by clicking on this link:

Leave your review here. Thank you!

I take reviews seriously and always look at them. This way, you are helping me provide you better content that you will LOVE in the future. A review doesn't have to be long, just one or two sentences and a number of stars you find appropriate (hopefully 5 of course).

Also, if I think your review is useful, I will mark it as "helpful." This will help you become more known on Amazon as a decent reviewer, and will ensure that more authors will contact you with free e-books in the future. This is how we can help each other.

76774680R00044

Made in the USA
Middletown, DE
15 June 2018